VOCAL SELECTIONS

Music by
PAUL McKIBBINS
BT McNICHOLL
Based on the Paramount Picture "IT"

The it girl

PAUL McKIBBINS (Music) has had performances by the New York Philharmonic, Cincinnati Pops, Alvin Ailey, New York Pops and many others. He was Composer-In-Residence at the University of Bridgeport (1986-1990). Television work includes *The Muppets* (Emmy nomination) and *The Sunshine Boys*. He produced music for the films *Unzipped* and *Suspicion*. He co-conceived and arranged *I Hear Music! Songs of Burton Lane* and created the ballets *Suite of Night Waltzes* (with Ann Reinking) and *Morgause* (with Courtney Conner). Recordings include *Follies* (1998, producer), *Setting Standards* (producer/arranger), Suite of Dances from *West Side Story* (arranger) and many instrumentals. He is the music administrator for Stephen Sondheim, Kander & Ebb, Maltby & Shire and Wright & Forrest and earned his Bachelor and Master of Music degrees from Manhattan School of Music.

BT McNICHOLL (Lyrics) won a national award from BMI for his first musical, based on *Cyrano*. He has written special material for IBM, as well as numerous magazine articles and cover stories. As a director, he has been associated with James Lapine, Jerry Zaks and Sam Mendes on a number of Broadway musicals, including the long-running revival of Kander & Ebb's *Cabaret*. Winner of a Drama League grant, McNicholl has directed new works at the Eugene O'Neill Theatre Center and, with Stephen Sondheim and Paul Gemignani, adapted *A Little Night Music* for the concert stage. In New York, he worked with Comden & Green on reviving their musical *Billion Dollar Baby*, starring Kristin Chenoweth, also producing the show's critically acclaimed cast album.

ORIGINAL CAST RECORDING AVAILABLE ON JAY RECORDS

Visit *The IT Girl* at www.itgirlmusical.com

EXCLUSIVELY DISTRIBUTED BY

HAL•LEONARD®
CORPORATION

CARLIN AMERICA

7777 W. BLUEMOUND RD. P.O. BOX 13819 MILWAUKEE, WI 53213

All photos by CAROL ROSEGG • Cover Illustration by GREGG COOK • Book & Cover Design by MICHAEL HOLMES

Visit Hal Leonard Online at www.halleonard.com

Black And White World

from the Musical The IT Girl

Lyrics by
BT McNICHOLL

Music by
PAUL McKIBBINS

3

Poco moto (♩ = 124)

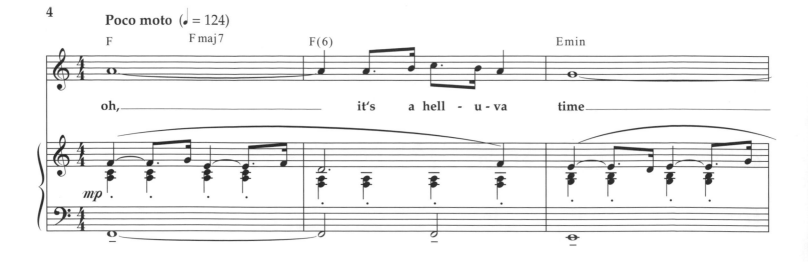

oh, _____ it's a hell - u - va time _____

_ Guns, per - ver - sion and crime on the street _ (Hey, a crook's got - ta eat!) _ We're

lost, _____ with our mor - als at sea.

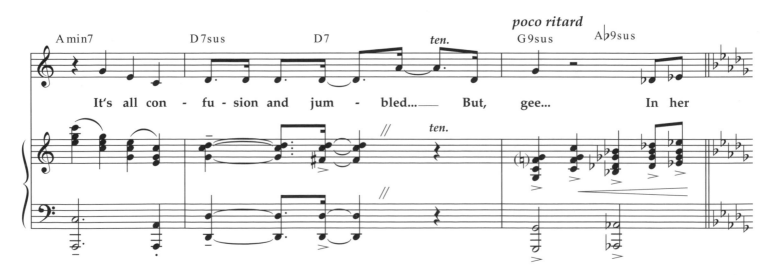

It's all con - fu - sion and jum - bled... But, gee... In her

Con poco moto

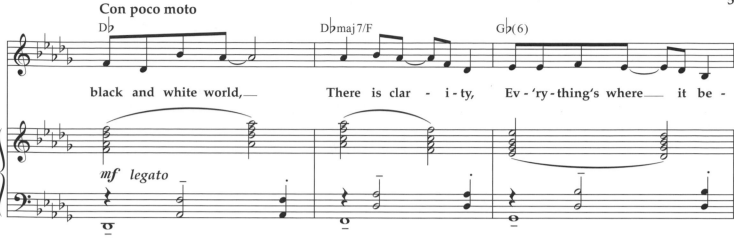

black and white world,___ There is clar - i - ty, Ev - 'ry-thing's where___ it be -

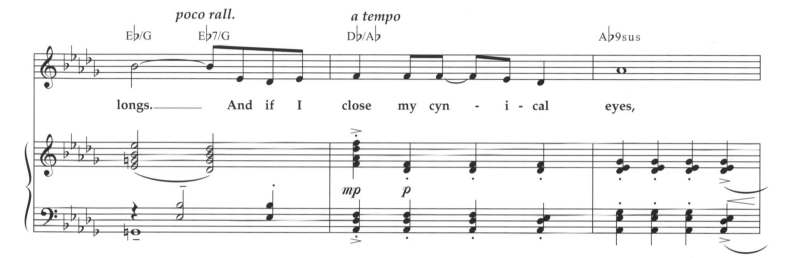

longs.___ And if I close my cyn - i - cal eyes,

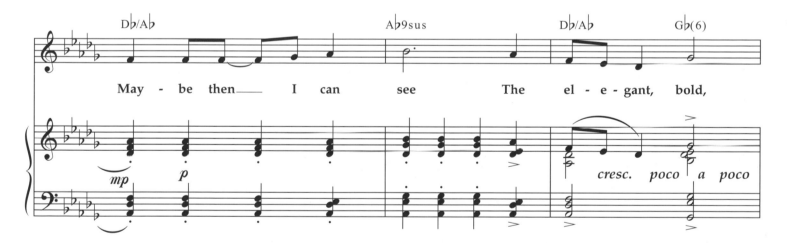

May - be then___ I can see The el - e - gant, bold,

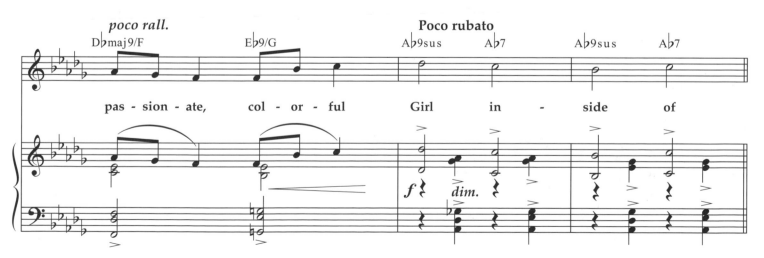

pas - sion - ate, col - or - ful Girl in - side of

6

Misterioso

Con moto

A poco moderato

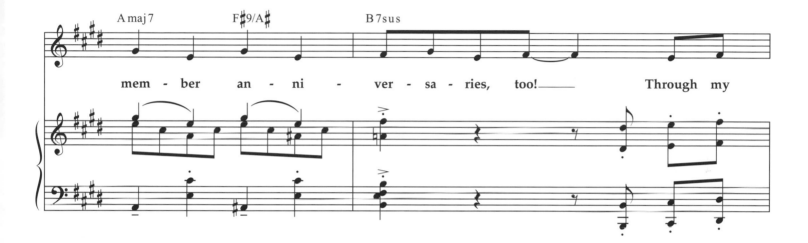

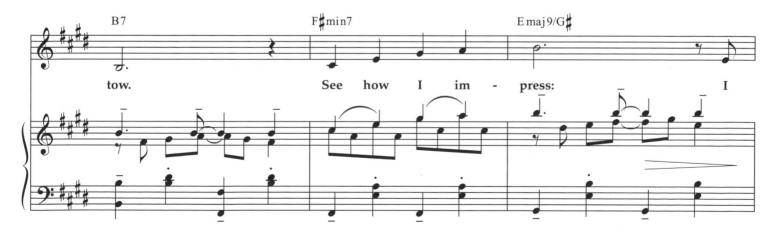

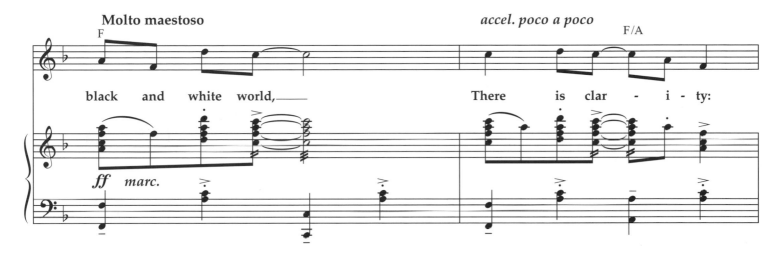

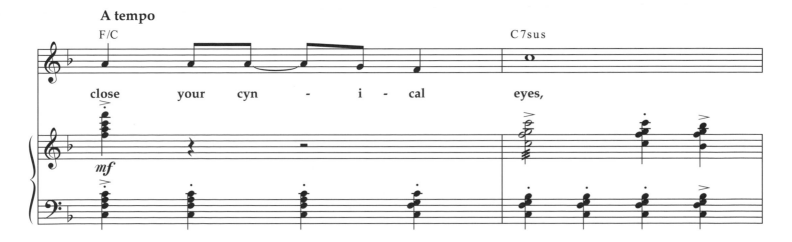

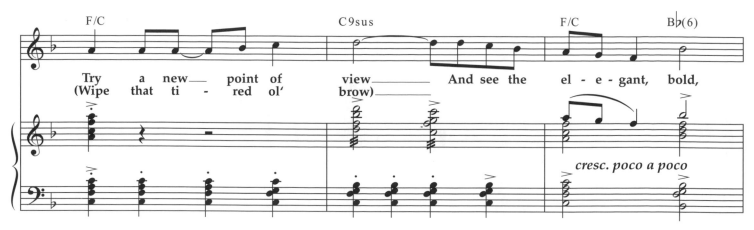

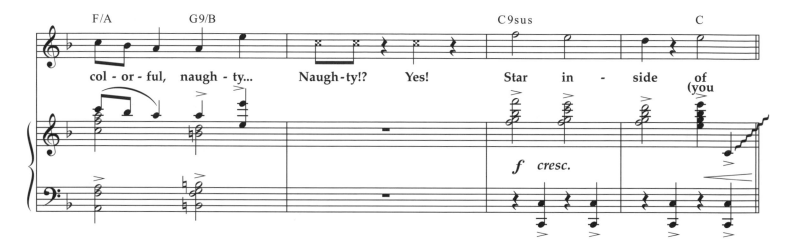

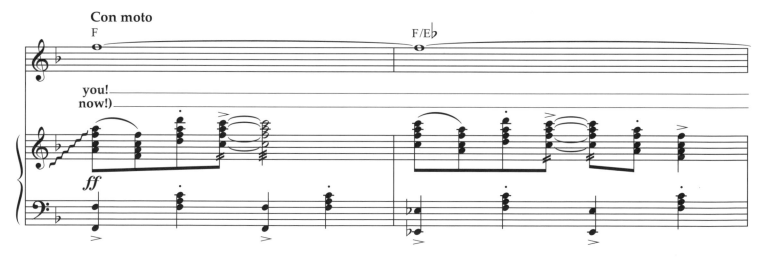

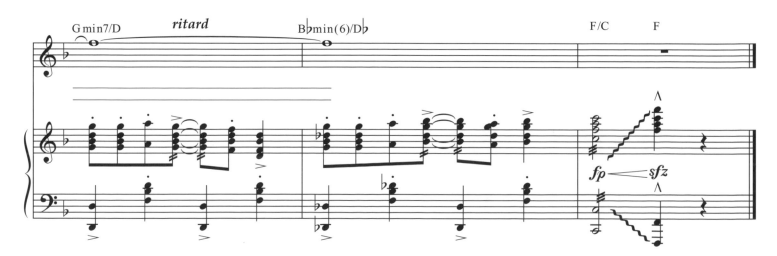

Why Not?
from the Musical The IT Girl

Lyrics by
BT McNICHOLL

Music by
PAUL McKIBBINS

Agitato con fuoco (♩ = 128)

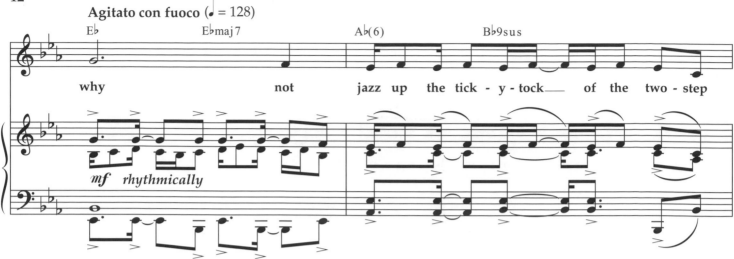

why ____ not jazz up the tick - y - tock ____ of the two - step

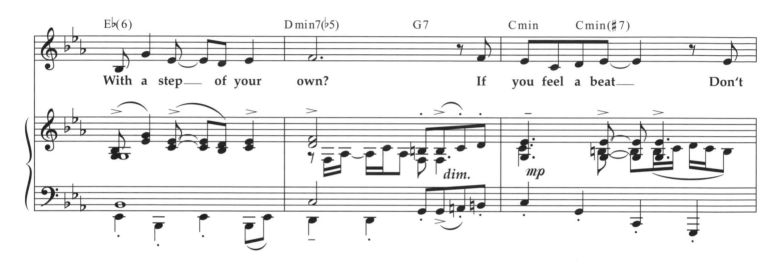

With a step ____ of your own? If you feel a beat ____ Don't

simp - ly re - peat ____ But lis-ten to what's dan-cey In your fan-ci - ful feet. Oh,

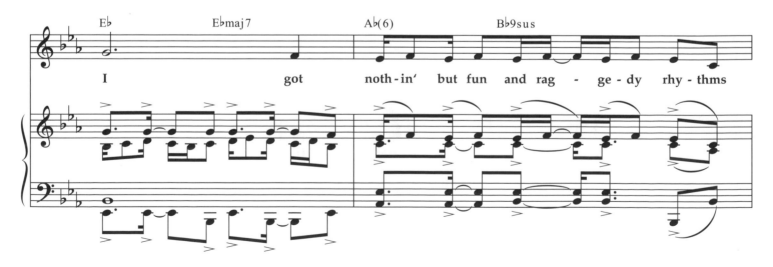

I got noth-in' but fun and rag - ge - dy rhy - thms

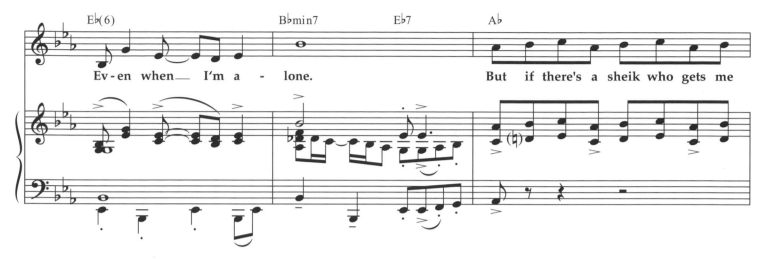

Ev-en when— I'm a - lone.
But if there's a sheik who gets me

car-ried a-way,— Rich or poor, Don't be sure He would-n't say:— "Oh,

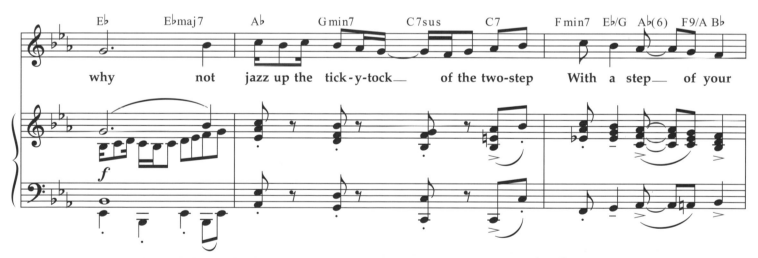

why not jazz up the tick-y-tock— of the two-step With a step— of your

own?!" My

Rubato

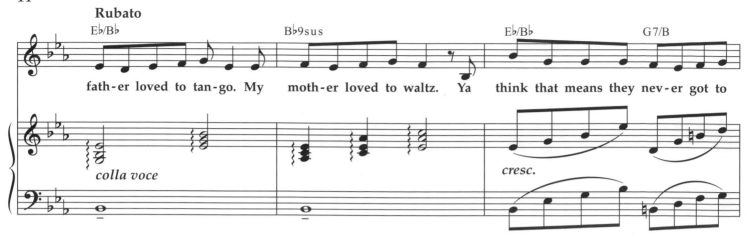

fath-er loved to tan-go. My moth-er loved to waltz. Ya think that means they nev-er got to

colla voce   *cresc.*

ad lib.   **Jazzy swing**   **Rubato**

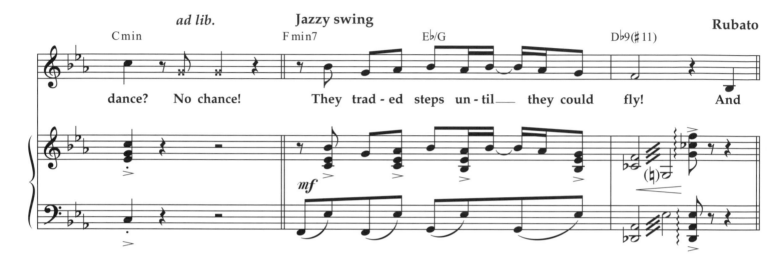

dance? No chance! They trad-ed steps un-til— they could fly! And

mf

con moto   *ritard*   *ten.*

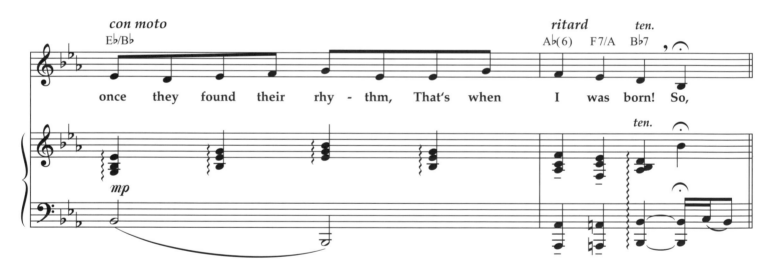

once they found their rhy-thm, That's when I was born! So,

mp   *ten.*

Agitato con fuoco

why not wind up the win-some wag— of the one-step

mf *rhythmically*

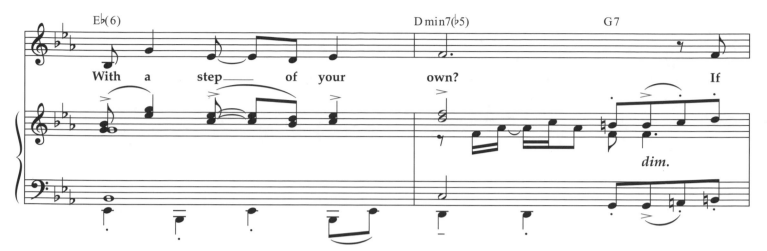

With a step___ of your own? If

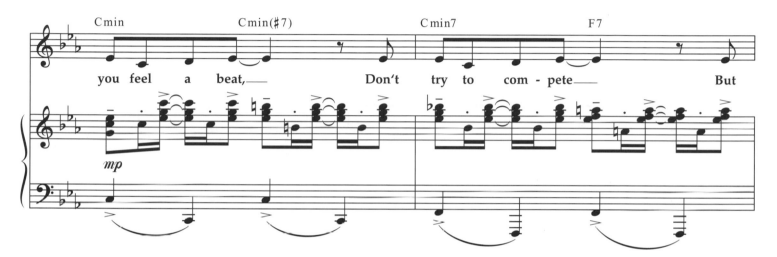

you feel a beat,___ Don't try to com - pete___ But

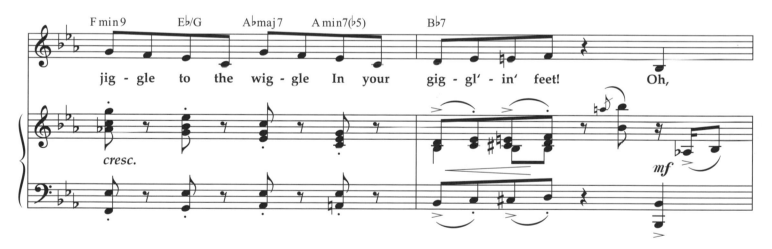

jig - gle to the wig - gle In your gig - gl'-in' feet! Oh,

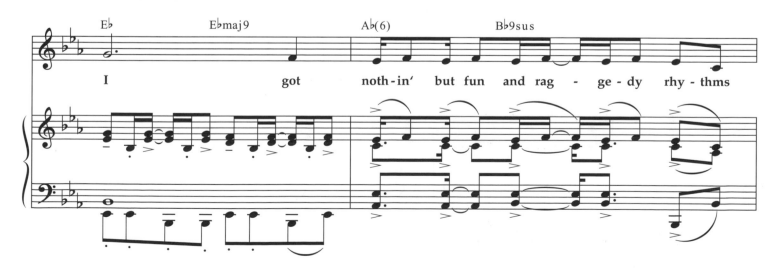

I got noth-in' but fun and rag - ge - dy rhy - thms

Ev - en when ___ I'm a - lone.

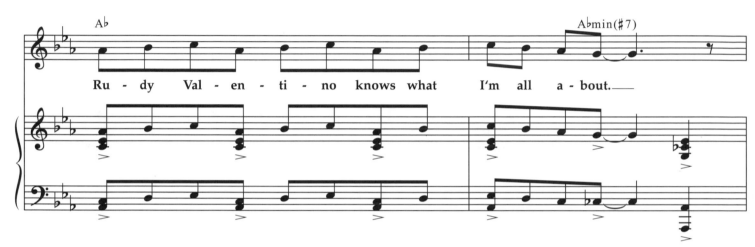

Ru - dy Val - en - ti - no knows what I'm all a - bout. ___

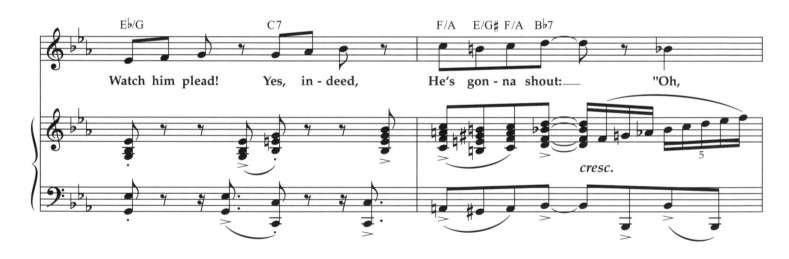

Watch him plead! Yes, in - deed, He's gon - na shout: ___ "Oh,

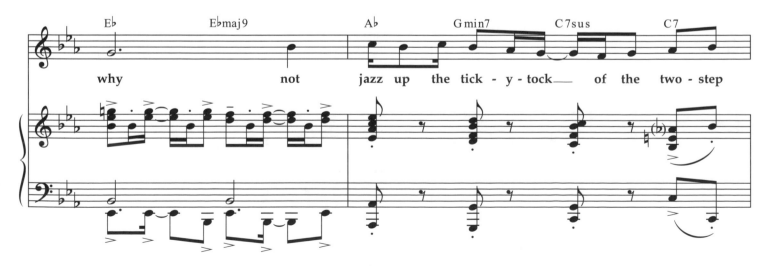

why not jazz up the tick - y - tock ___ of the two - step

With a step— of your own?" So

what if they say he's out— of my reach? I'll nev-er stop un-til— I can teach him

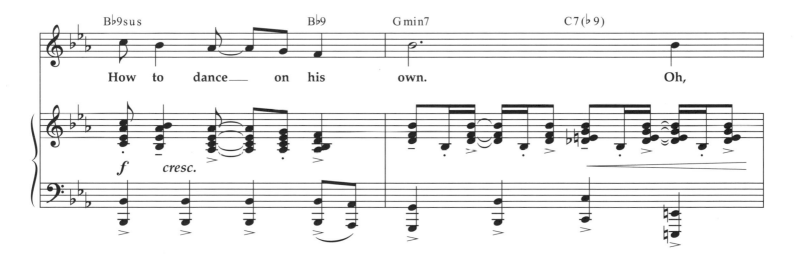

How to dance— on his own. Oh,

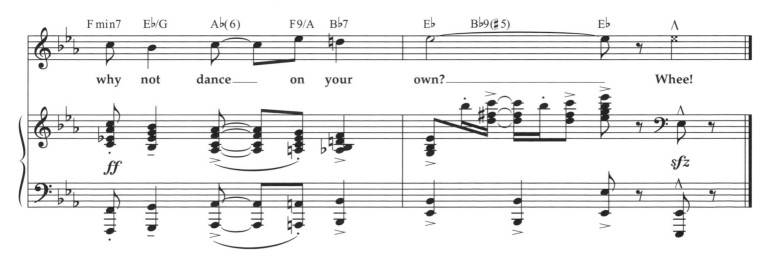

why not dance— on your own?— Whee!

IT

from the Musical The IT Girl

Lyrics by
BT McNICHOLL

Music by
PAUL McKIBBINS

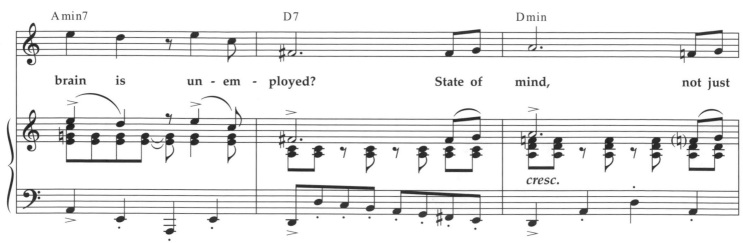

brain is un- em- ployed? State of mind, not just

phys- i- cal beau- ty, Is what leaves 'em ov- er- joyed! Like Freud says:

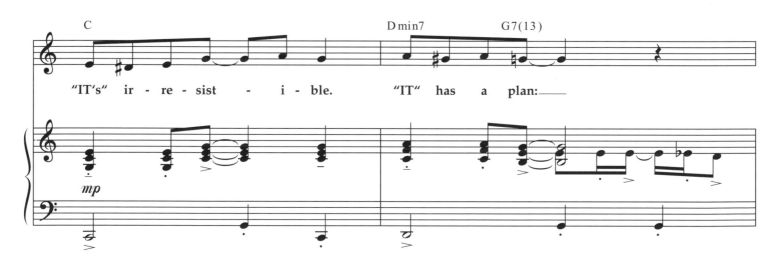

"IT's" ir- re- sist- i- ble. "IT" has a plan:____

Men win the la- dies, and la- dies the man!____ Oh, ya

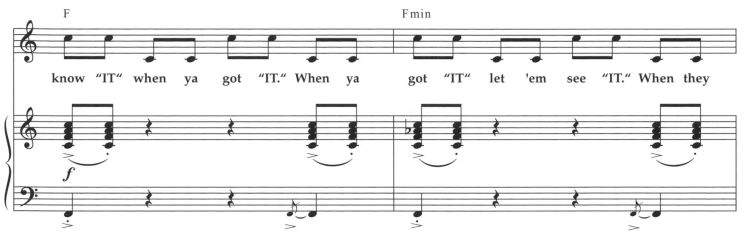

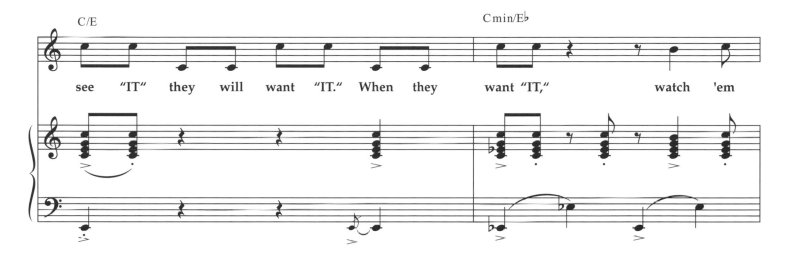

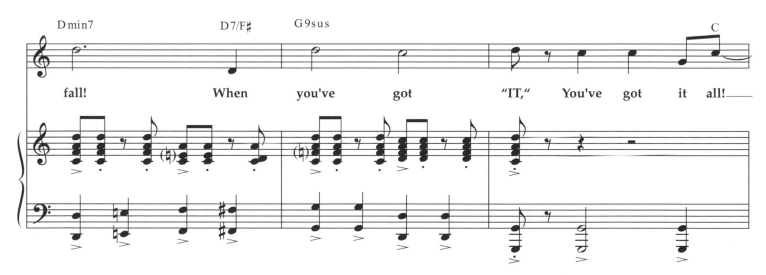

A bit slower

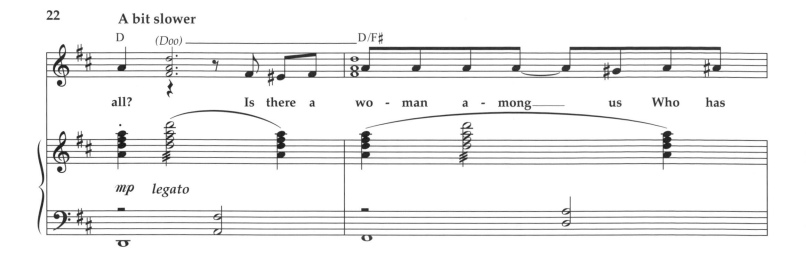

all? Is there a wo - man a - mong——— us Who has

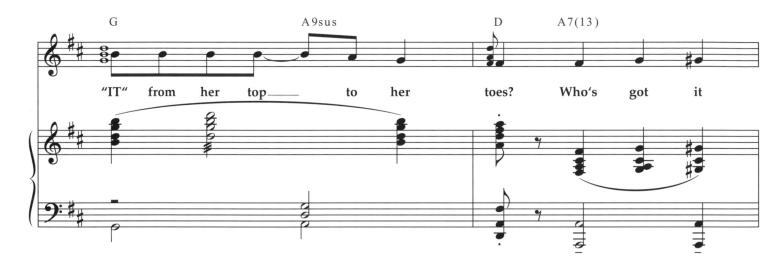

"IT" from her top——— to her toes? Who's got it

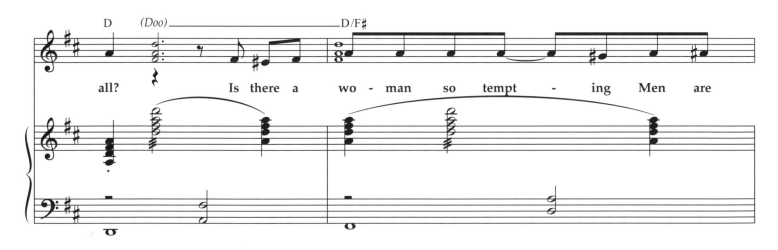

all? Is there a wo - man so tempt - ing Men are

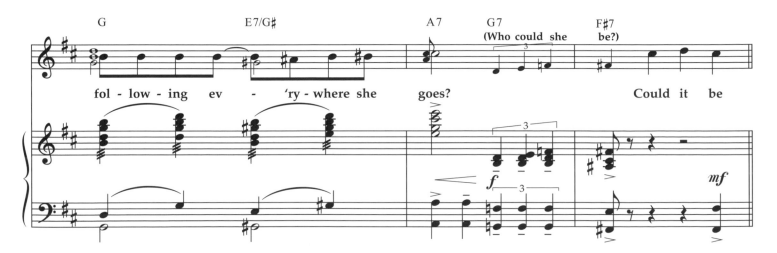

fol - low - ing ev - 'ry - where she goes? Could it be

A Tempo I

her? Or may-be her? I want to know! I want to find that girl Who'd

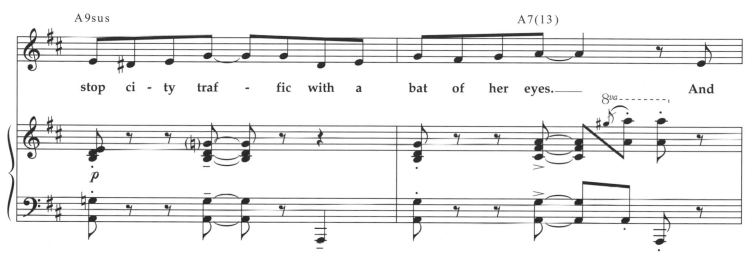

stop ci-ty traf - fic with a bat of her eyes.___ And

get men so hot___ they have to loos-en their ties.___ A

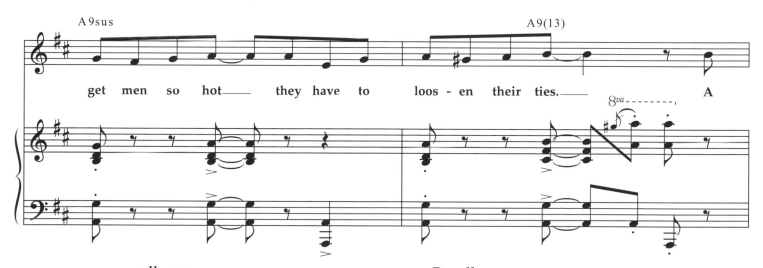

rall. poco a poco **Broadly**

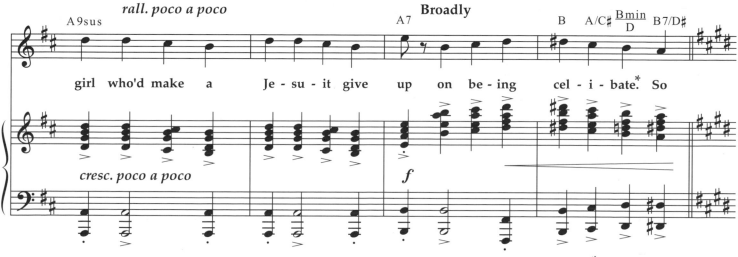

girl who'd make a Je-su-it give up on be-ing cel-i-bate.* So

* (pronounced: sell - a - bit)

Cakewalk

accel. poco a poco

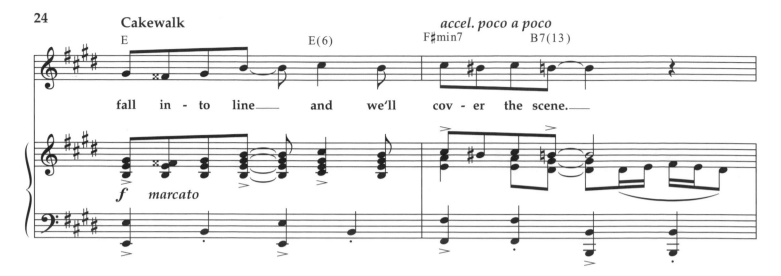

fall in - to line____ and we'll cov - er the scene.____

Let's find The "IT"____ Girl and make her a queen.____ Oh, ya

A tempo

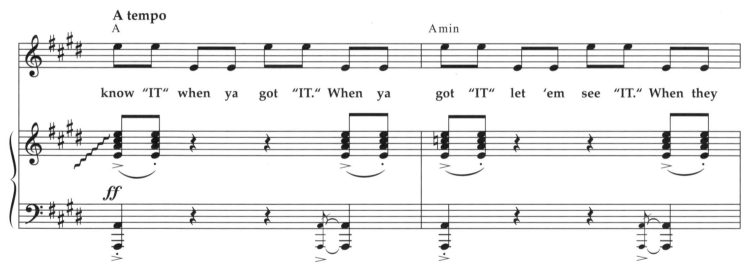

know "IT" when ya got "IT." When ya got "IT" let 'em see "IT." When they

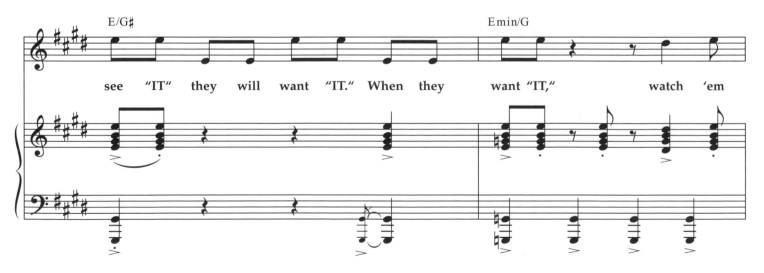

see "IT" they will want "IT." When they want "IT," watch 'em

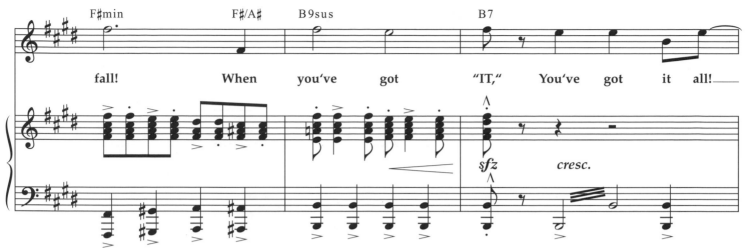

fall! When you've got "IT," You've got it all!____

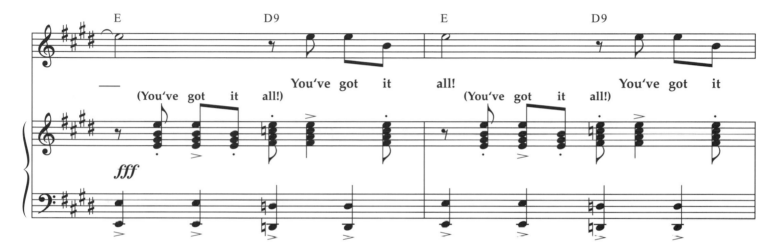

____ (You've got it all!) You've got it all! (You've got it all!) You've got it

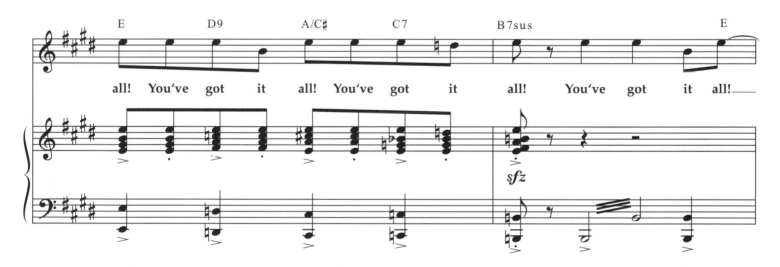

all! You've got it all! You've got it all! You've got it all!____

Mama's Arms

from the Musical **The IT Girl**

Lyrics by
BT McNICHOLL

Music by
PAUL McKIBBINS

A Perfect Plan
from the Musical The IT Girl

Lyrics by
BT McNICHOLL

Music by
PAUL McKIBBINS

ADELA:
Artists or millionaires-- what's the difference? Whenever I set a foolproof trap to catch a man, it's always the same problem: The other woman.

I try sabotaging her and *she* ends up winning the prize.
That's how I lost my Frenchman, Charles... Ah, Charles...

doc-tored up her sketch-ings With some etch-ings of my own. To show her lack of skill

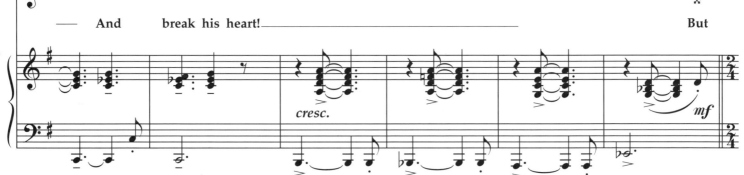

— And break his heart! But

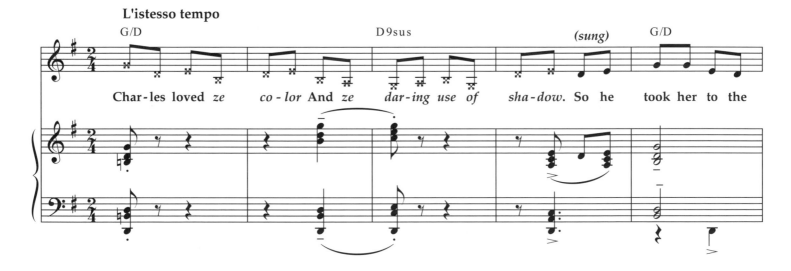

L'istesso tempo

Char-les loved *ze co-lor* And *ze dar-ing use of sha-dow.* So he took her to the

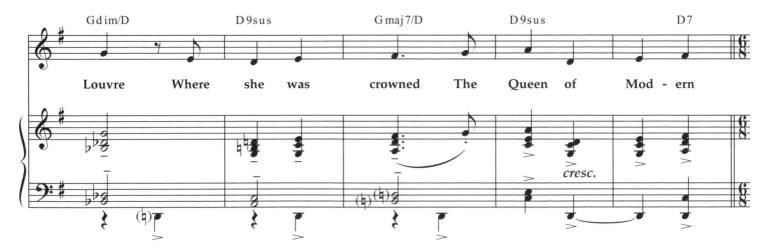

Louvre Where she was crowned The Queen of Mod-ern

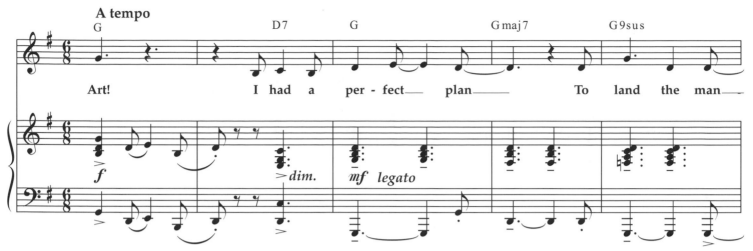

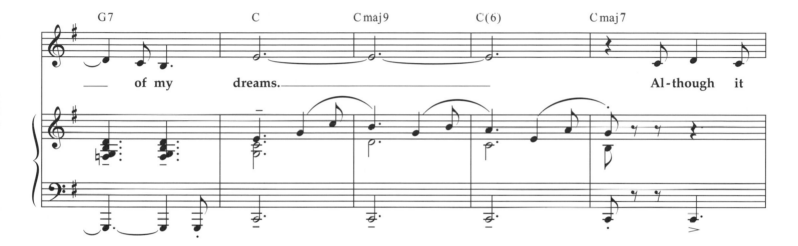

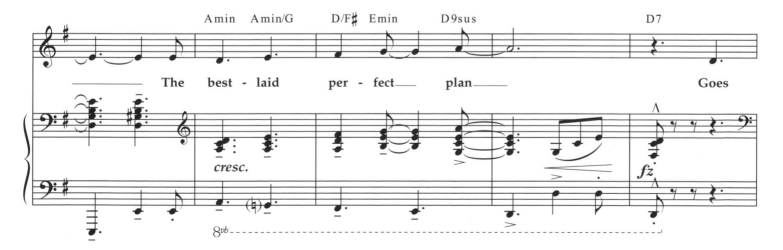

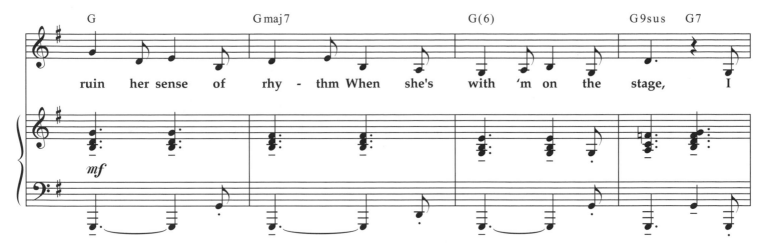

ruin her sense of rhy - thm When she's with 'm on the stage, I

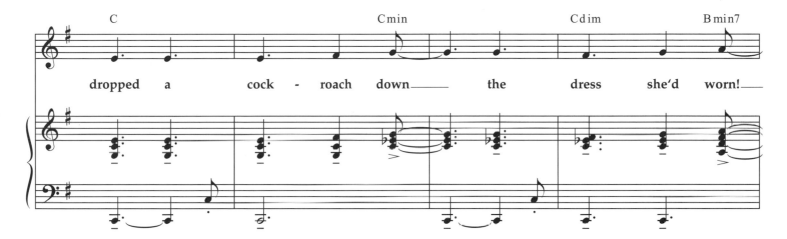

dropped a cock - roach down_____ the dress she'd worn!_____

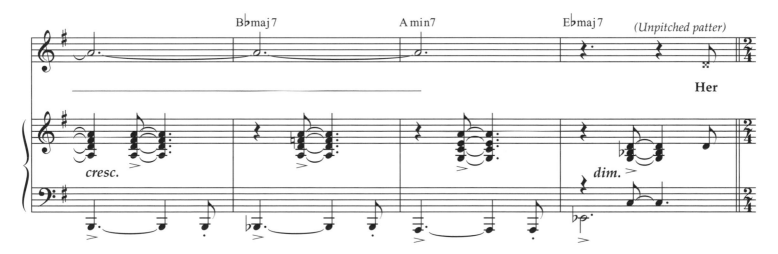

(Unpitched patter)

Her

L'istesso tempo

bo - dy start - ed jerk - ing And her feet be - gan a - twist - ing, So he

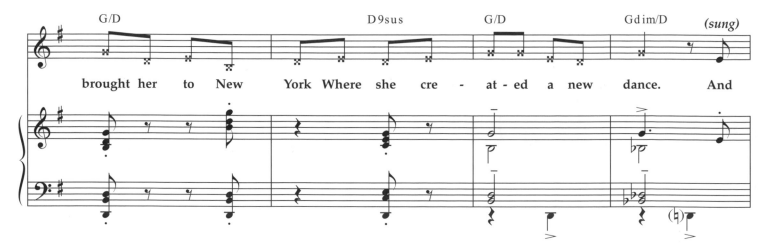

brought her to New York Where she cre - at - ed a new dance. And

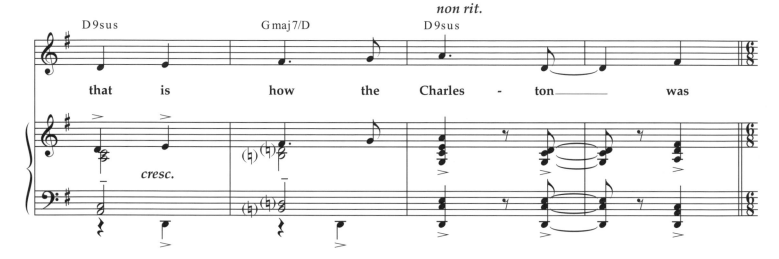

that is how the Charles - ton was

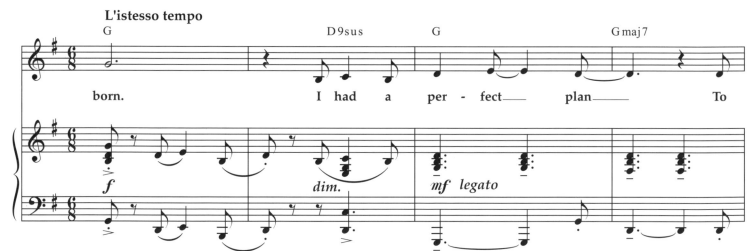

born. I had a per - fect plan To

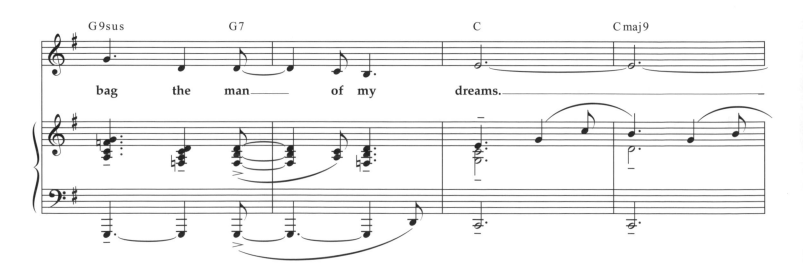

bag the man of my dreams.

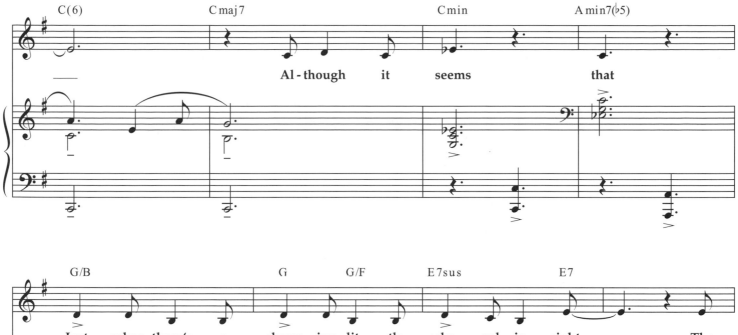

Al-though it seems that

Just when there's a charm-ing lit-tle cha-pel in sight,_____ The

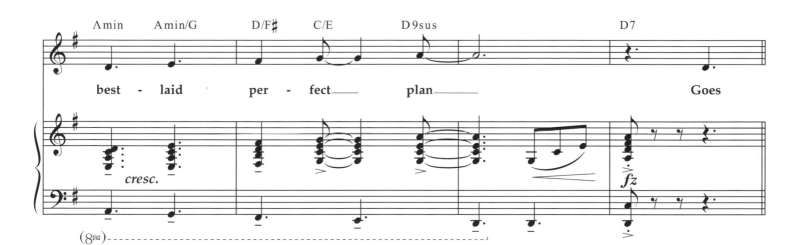

best - laid per - fect_____ plan_____ Goes

Flowing, l'istesso tempo

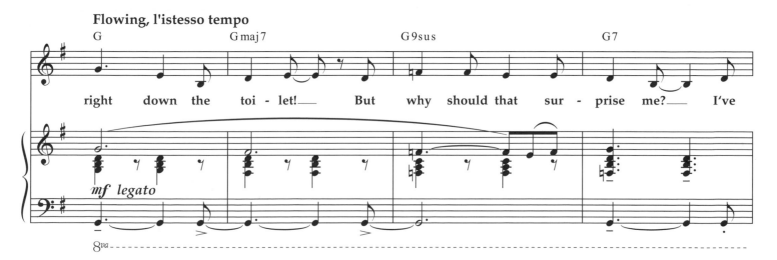

right down the toi - let!_____ But why should that sur - prise me?_____ I've

learned it on my___ own. (I went to night school.)___

A min7   **D**

cresc.

(8va)

G   **E♭**   **F**   **G**   **E♭**   **F**

(spoken) Then I had one final affair. *(cont'd)*

mf rhythmically

8va

A♭   **F♭**   **G♭**   **A♭**   **F♭**   **G♭**

But *this* time it was with a real man ... my Italian Stallion -- Louie.

(8va)

A♭   **A♭maj7**   **A♭(6)**   **A♭maj7**

(sung) Lou - ie was a life - guard, Who ruled the Riv - i - er - a. He'd

mp poco marcato

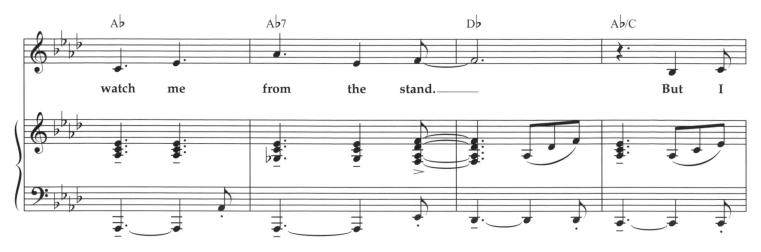

watch me from the stand._____ But I

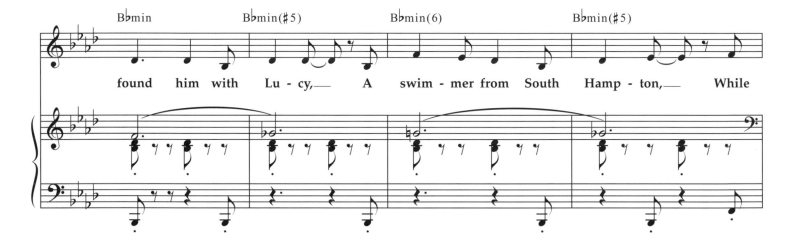

found him with Lu - cy,___ A swim - mer from South Hamp - ton,___ While

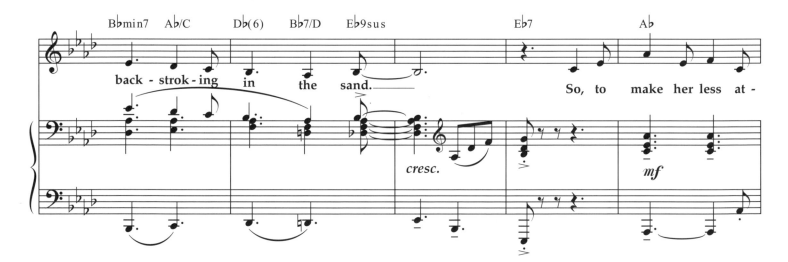

back - strok - ing in the sand.___ So, to make her less at -

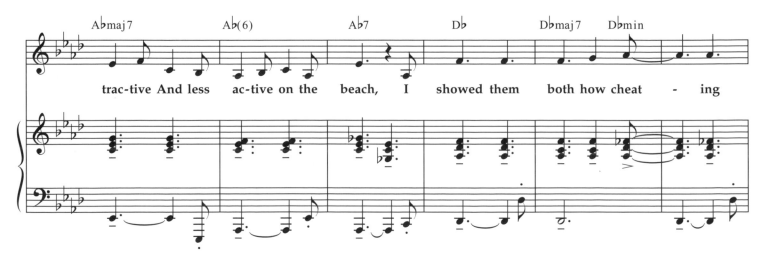

trac-tive And less ac-tive on the beach, I showed them both how cheat - ing

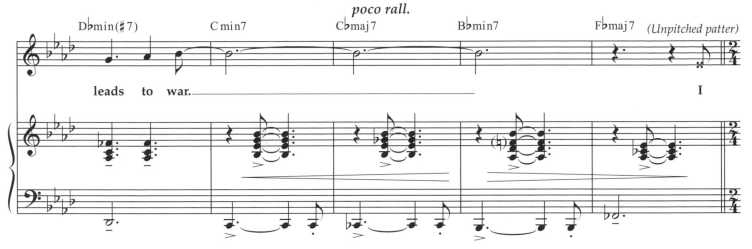

leads to war._____ I

put a hand-some ac-tor in a tow-el in her bed-room. When Lou-ie caught him

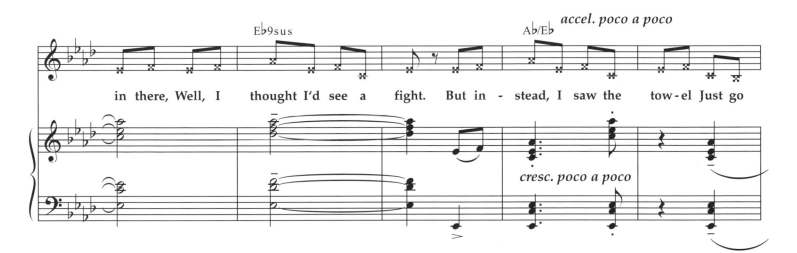

in there, Well, I thought I'd see a fight. But in-stead, I saw the tow-el Just go

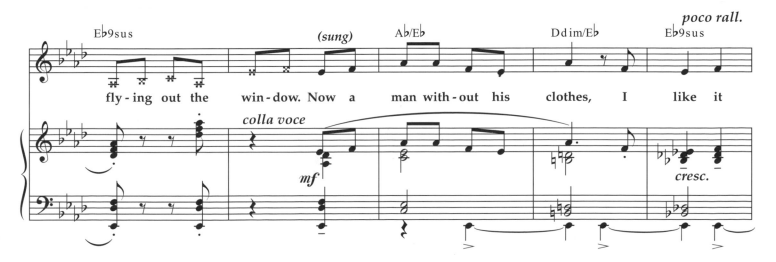

fly-ing out the win-dow. Now a man with-out his clothes, I like it

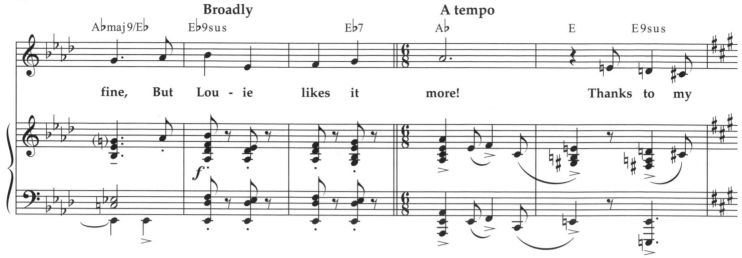

fine, But Lou - ie likes it more! Thanks to my

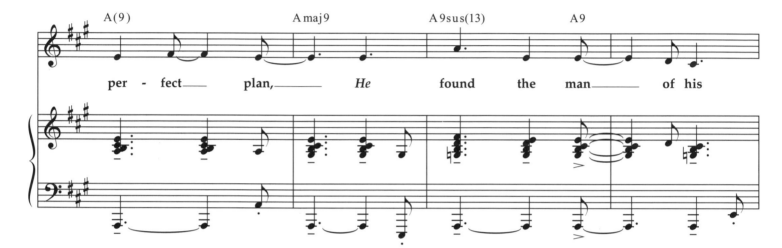

per - fect___ plan,___ *He* found the man___ of his

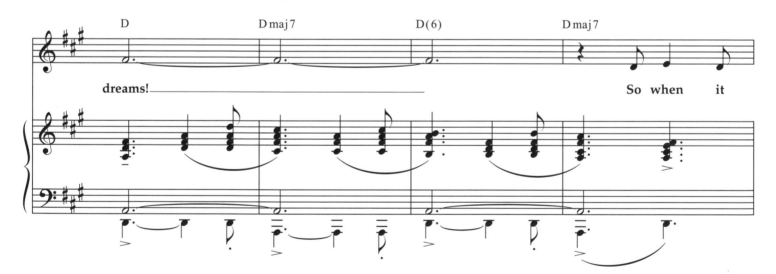

dreams!_____ So when it

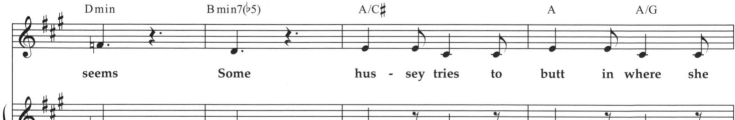

seems Some hus - sey tries to butt in where she

1.

5.

"Why not jazz up
the ticky-tock of
the two-step with a
step of your own?"

1. "How Do You Say…?"
2. Jean Louisa Kelly has IT!
3. Monte Wheeler, Danette Holden, Stephen DeRosa,
   Susan M. Haefner cut to The Chase
4. Jonathan Dokuchitz, Jean Louisa Kelly:
   "You're the Best Thing That Ever Happened to Me"
5. Susan M. Haefner, Jean Louisa Kelly,
   Danette Holden: "Why Not?"

Looking everywhere —
and no sign
of IT anywhere!

4.

3.

2.

Coney Island

from the Musical The IT Girl

Lyrics by
BT McNICHOLL

Music by
PAUL McKIBBINS

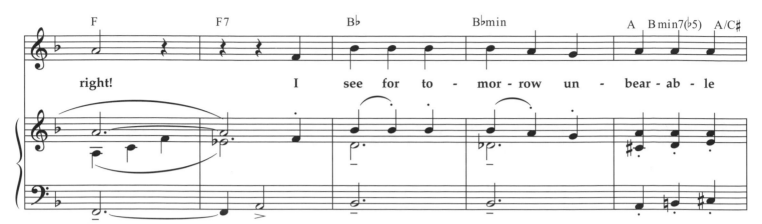

right! I see for to - mor - row un - bear - ab - le

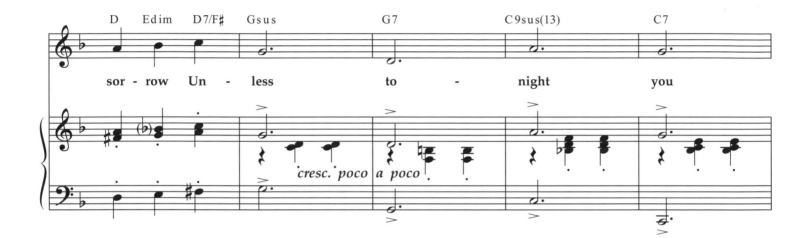

sor - row Un - less to - night you

cresc. poco a poco

MAN:

Run to play on the Mid - way. There's the o - cean! I can

mf

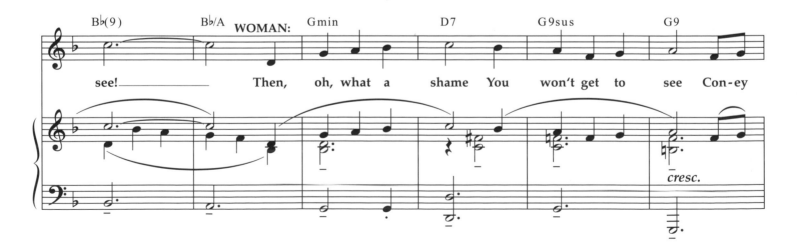

WOMAN:

see!_____ Then, oh, what a shame You won't get to see Con - ey

cresc.

Is - land_____ with me.   La

la la la la la la la.   **WOMAN:** Go on sing it!   **MAN:** Well, I

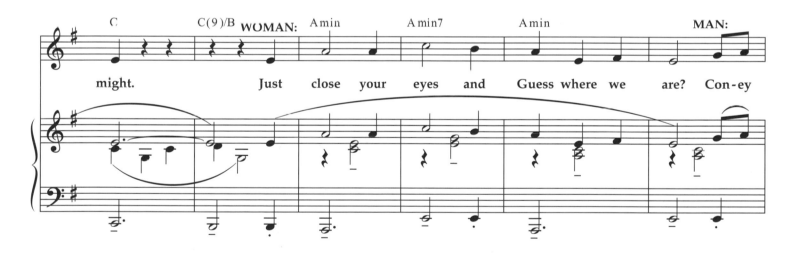

might.   **WOMAN:** Just close your eyes and   Guess where we are? Con-ey   **MAN:**

Is - land_____ to - night!   **WOMAN:** Take your

tie off! Mess your hair up! Have your palm read. Do it

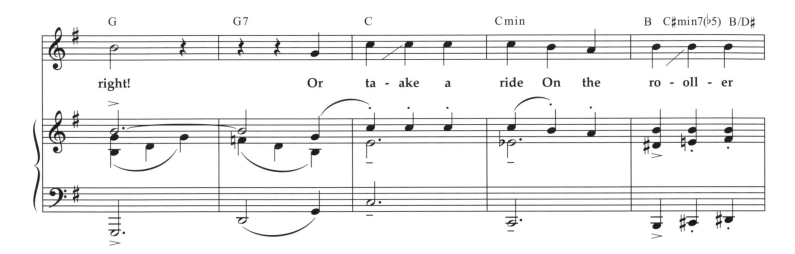

right! Or ta - ake a ride On the ro - oll - er

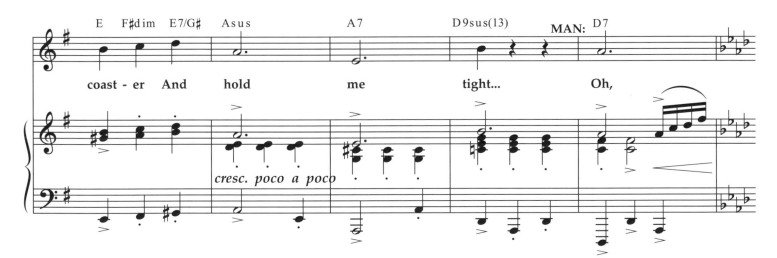

coast - er And hold me tight... **MAN:** Oh,

where the heck is the Mid - way?____ **WOMAN:** By the o - cean, On the

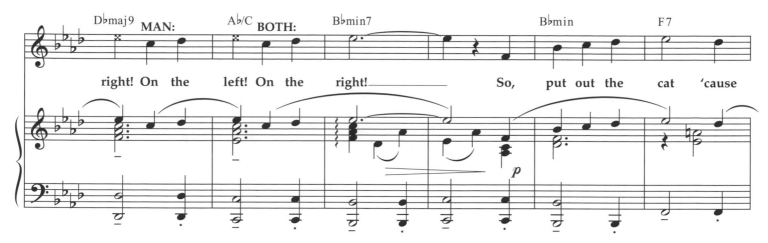

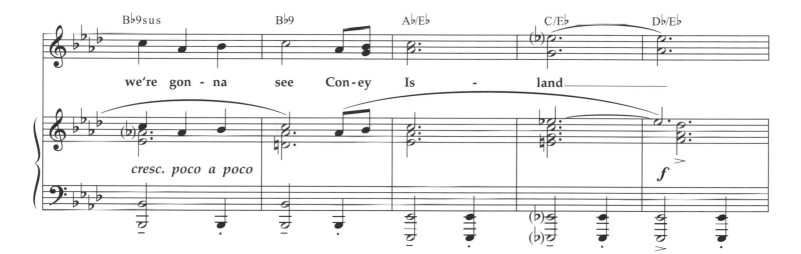

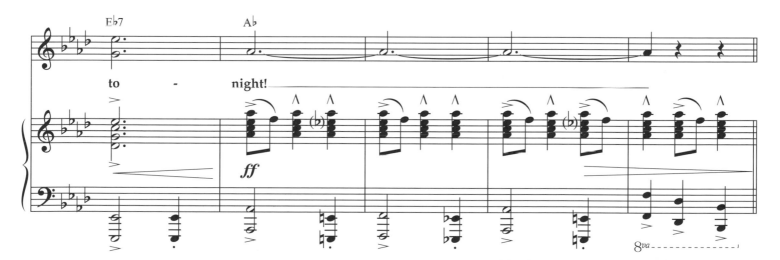

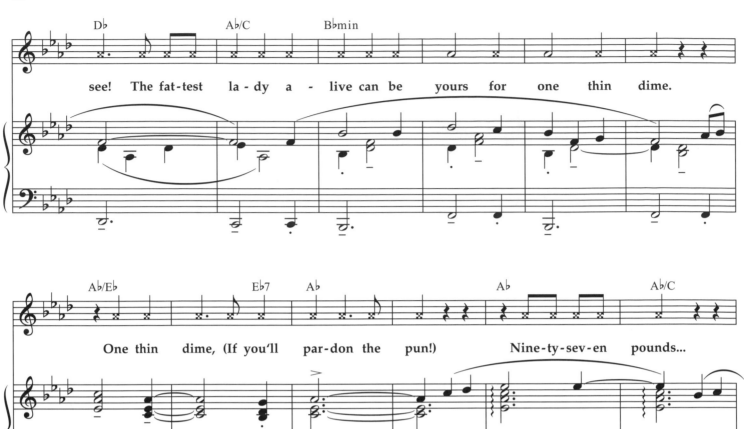

see! The fat-test la - dy a - live can be yours for one thin dime.

One thin dime, (If you'll par-don the pun!) Nine-ty-sev-en pounds...

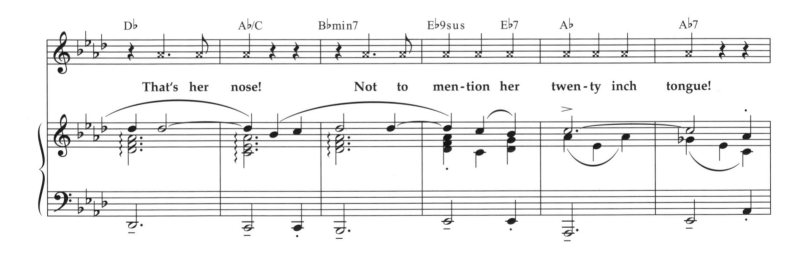

That's her nose! Not to men-tion her twen-ty inch tongue!

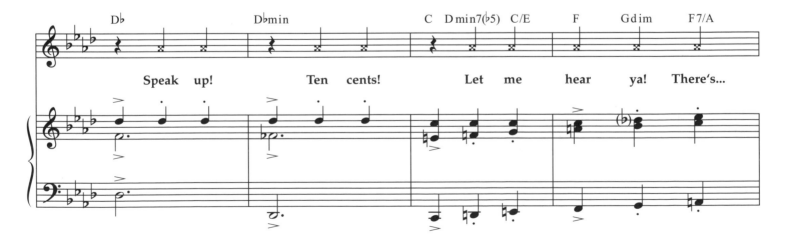

Speak up! Ten cents! Let me hear ya! There's...

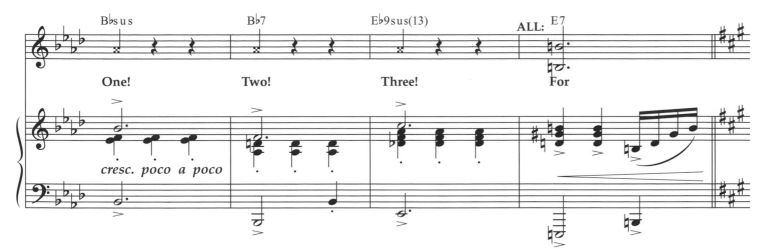

One! Two! Three! For

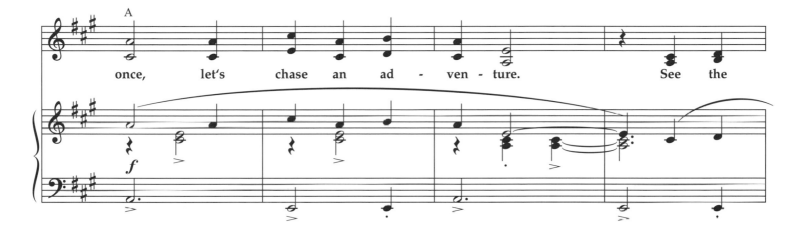

once, let's chase an ad - ven - ture. See the

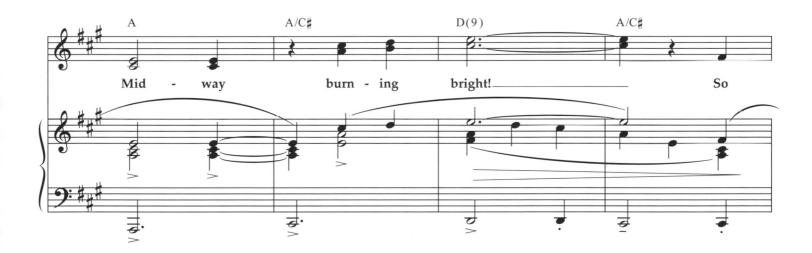

Mid - way burn - ing bright!_____ So

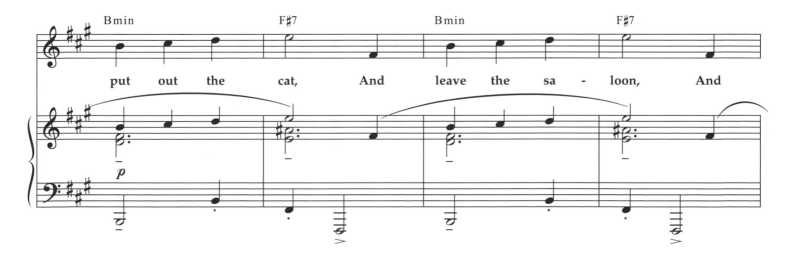

put out the cat, And leave the sa - loon, And

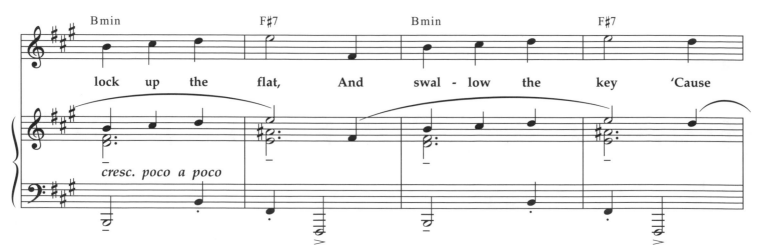

lock up the flat, And swal-low the key 'Cause

cresc. poco a poco

we're gon-na see Con-ey Is - land____ to -

ff

night!____

fff

sfz *sfz* *fp* *sffz*

Stay With Me

from the Musical The IT Girl

Lyrics by
BT McNICHOLL

Music by
PAUL McKIBBINS

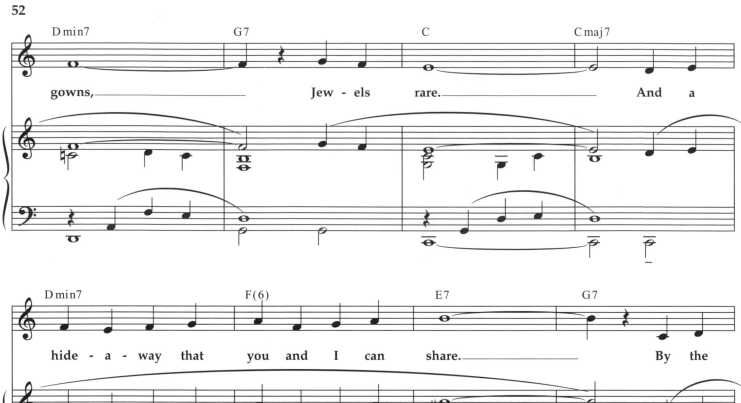

gowns,_____ Jew - els rare._____ And a

hide - a - way that you and I can share._____ By the

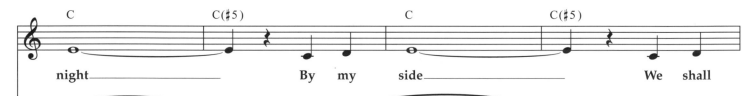

night_____ By my side_____ We shall

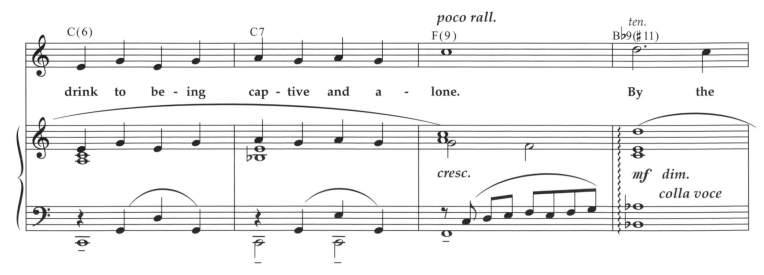

drink to be - ing cap - tive and a - lone. By the

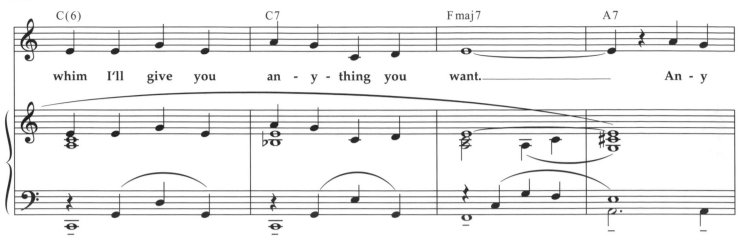

whim I'll give you an - y - thing you want. _____ An - y

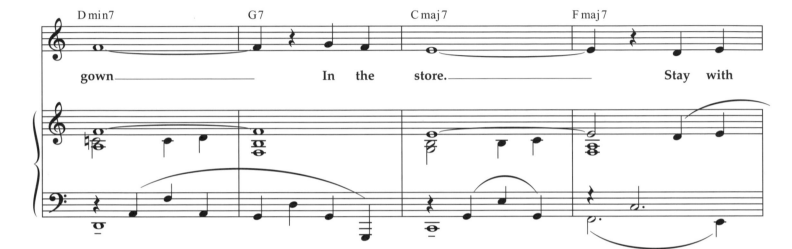

gown _____ In the store. _____ Stay with

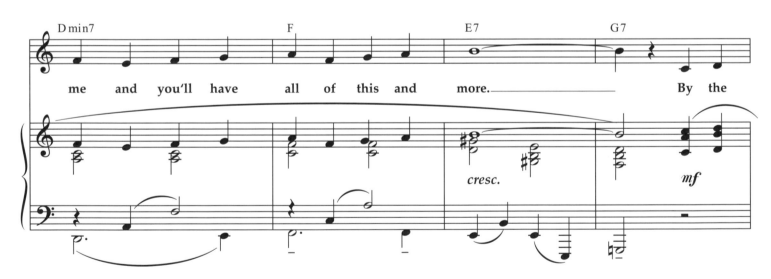

me and you'll have all of this and more. _____ By the

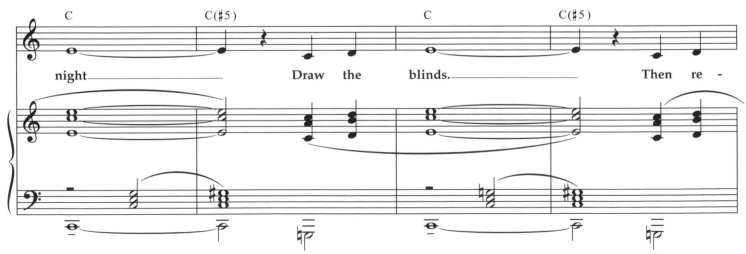

night _____ Draw the blinds. _____ Then re -

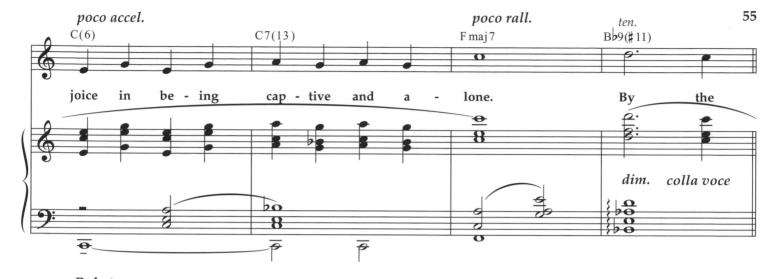

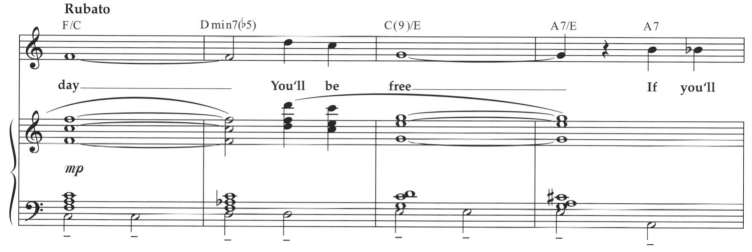

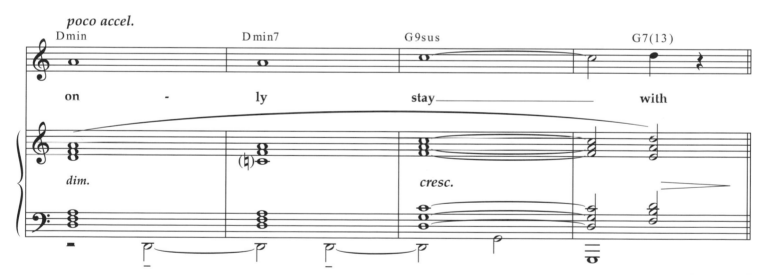

Left-Hand Arrangement

from the Musical **The IT Girl**

Lyrics by
BT McNICHOLL

Music by
PAUL McKIBBINS

*(pronounced: trin-kits)

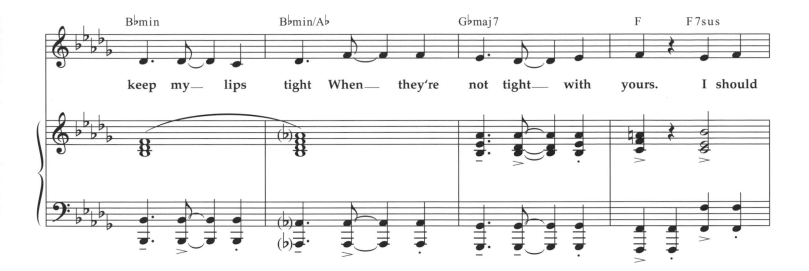

keep my— lips tight When— they're not tight— with yours. I should

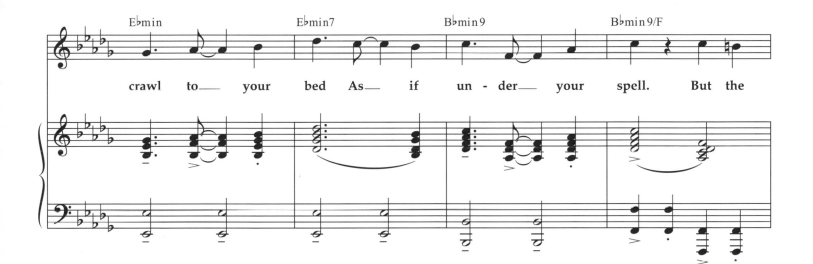

crawl to— your bed As— if un - der— your spell. But the

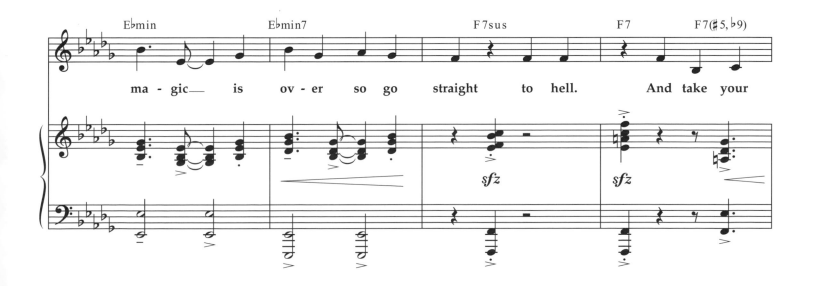

ma - gic— is ov - er so go straight to hell. And take your

60

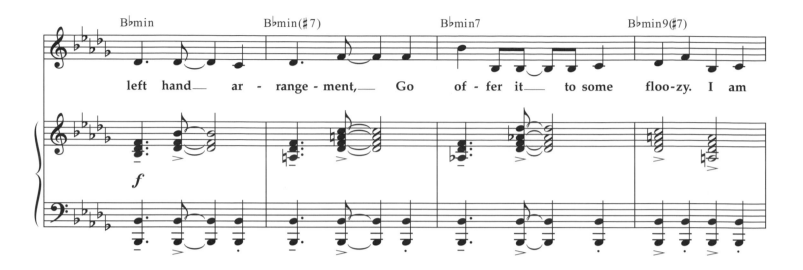

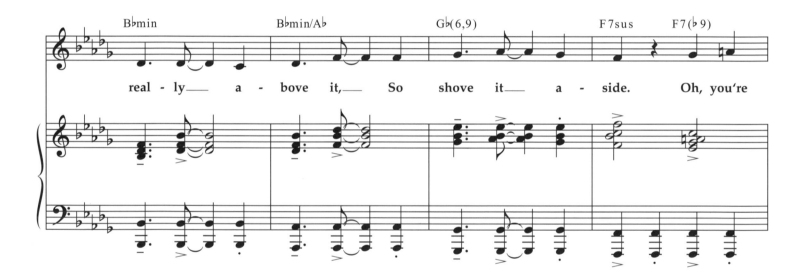

Step Into Their Shoes

from the Musical The IT Girl

Lyrics by
BT McNICHOLL

Music by
PAUL McKIBBINS

Steady rag

Step in-to our shoes, Then step out in our shoes. Go

down the road we trudge Be-fore you make a judge - ment.

Step in-to our shoes And you're li' - ble to say: "When

mak-in' friends, We dis-cov-er you can't judge a book By its cov - er." So,

step in - to our shoes And see it our way.

My

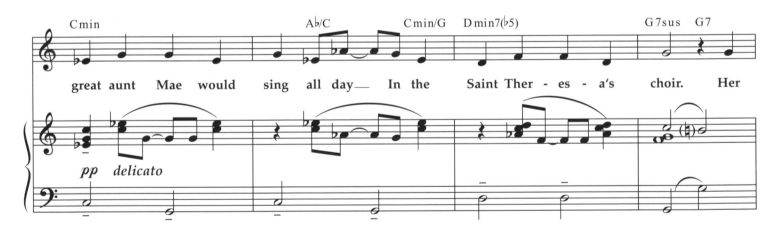

great aunt Mae would sing all day In the Saint Ther - es - a's choir. Her

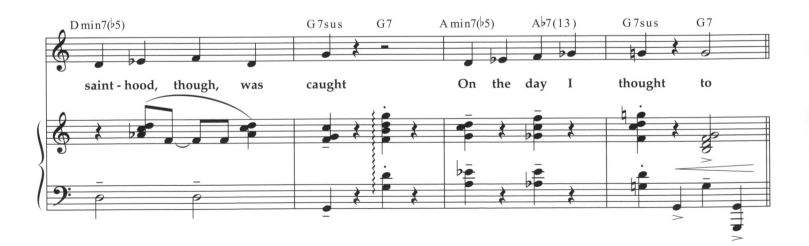

saint - hood, though, was caught On the day I thought to

A little brighter, rag

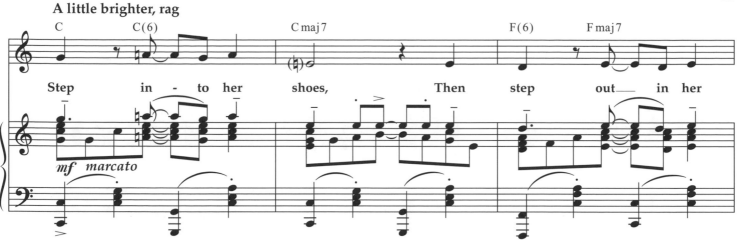

Step in - to her shoes, Then step out in her

shoes. I found she changed her tune When

li - quored up with moon - shine! Step in - to her

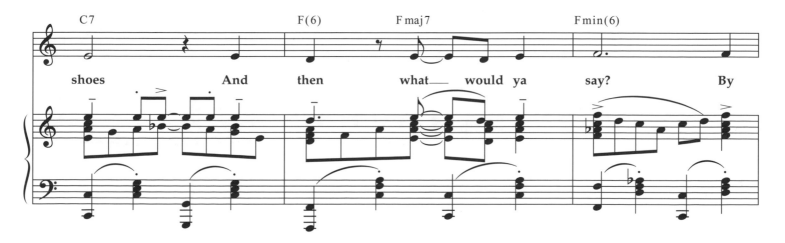

shoes And then what would ya say? By

day she seems ap-os-tol - ic, By night she be-comes al-co-hol - ic! So,

step in - to her shoes And see___ it her way! A dap - per young

swell With a vel - vet col - lar, Drives a Rolls, And is

free with a dol - lar. Looks as if he's set, But this

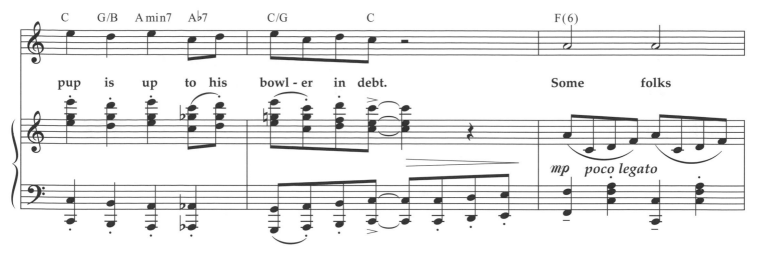

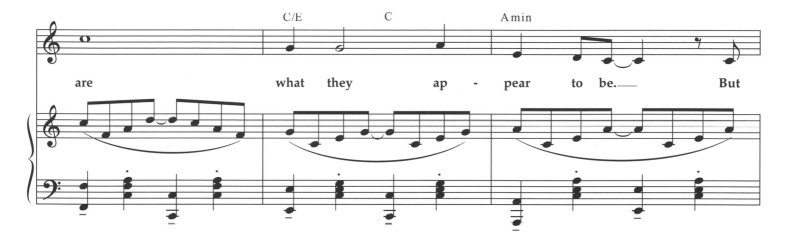

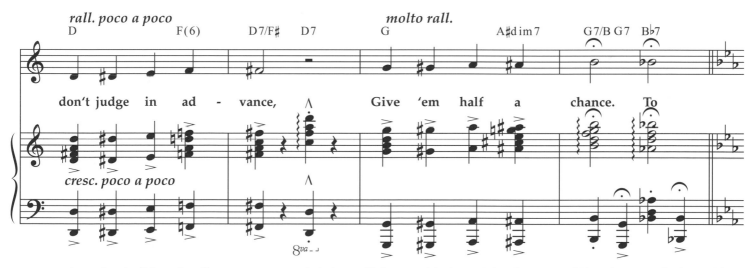

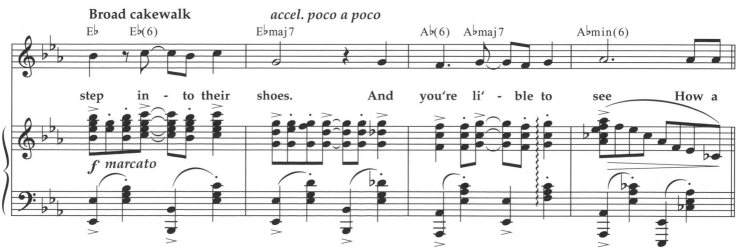

flash-y young buck__ may be down on his luck.__ A bum from the docks__ may be load-ed in stocks.__ A mi-ser-ly gram'-pa may own half-a Tam-pa,

But you'll nev-er know till ya Step in-to their shoes and see__ it their

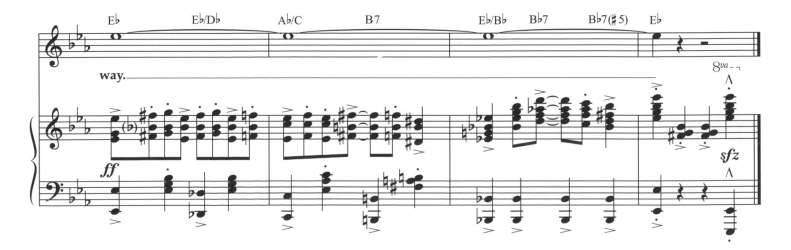

way._____

How Do You Say..?

from the Musical The IT Girl

Lyrics by
BT McNICHOLL

Music by
PAUL McKIBBINS

Quick, be-fore we reach our peak,— let's... *(snap, snap)* How do you say..?—

— You— know!

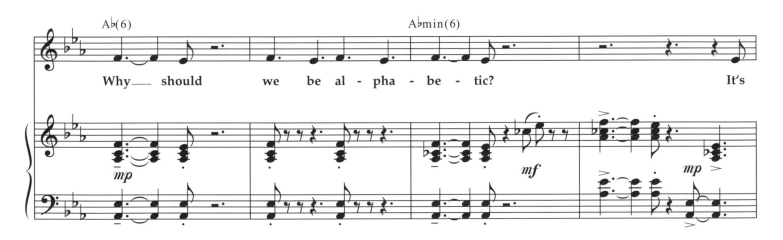

Why— should we be al-pha-be-tic? It's

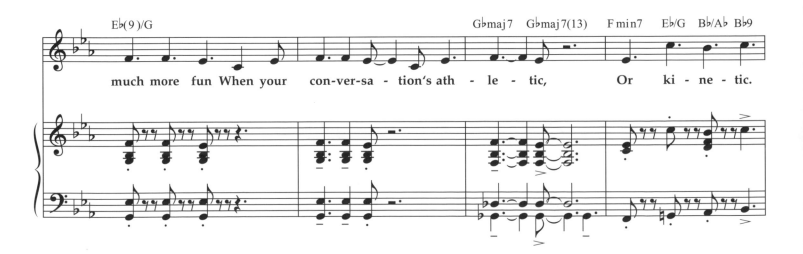

much more fun When your con-ver-sa-tion's ath-le-tic, Or ki-ne-tic.

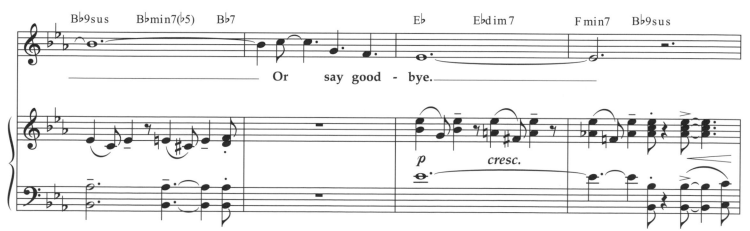

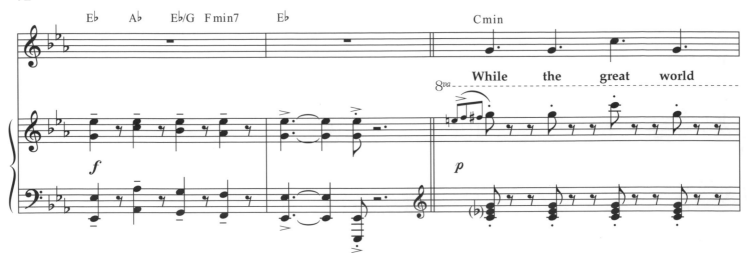

While the great world

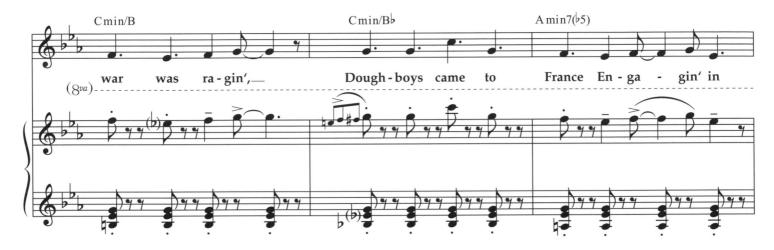

war was ra-gin',— Dough-boys came to France En-ga-gin' in

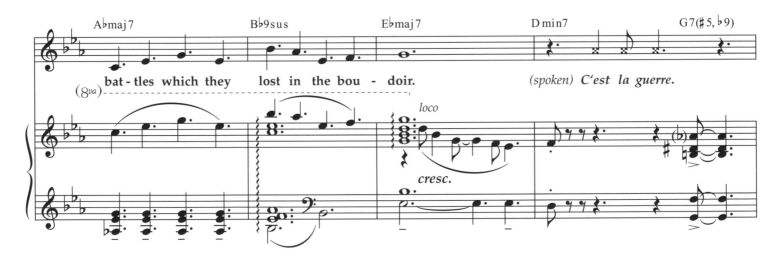

bat-tles which they lost in the bou-doir. *(spoken)* **C'est la guerre.**

(sung) Now they have re-turned from Par-is,— Speak-ing French with-

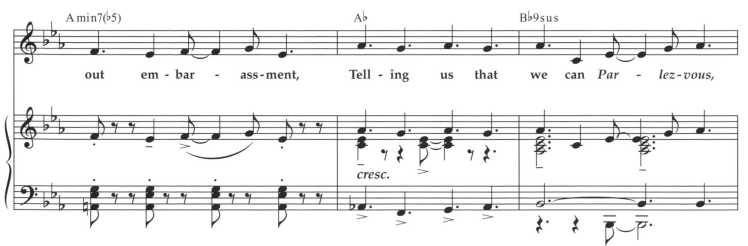

out em - bar - ass - ment, Tell - ing us that we can *Par - lez-vous,*

non ritard

too._____ So

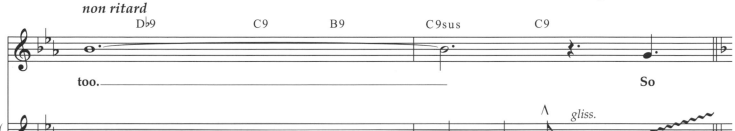

let's be bold, Ring the bell. Ev - 'ry swell and

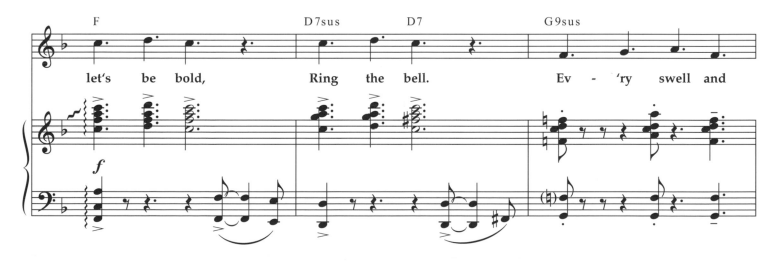

ne'er - do - well__ can...__ How do you say..?__

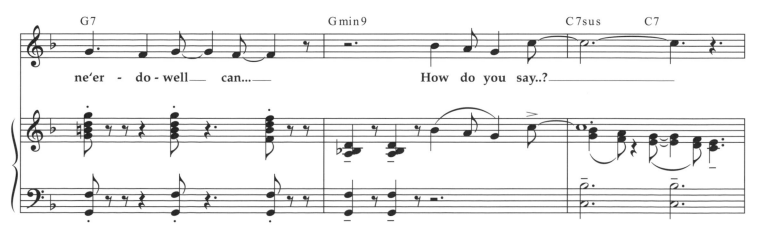

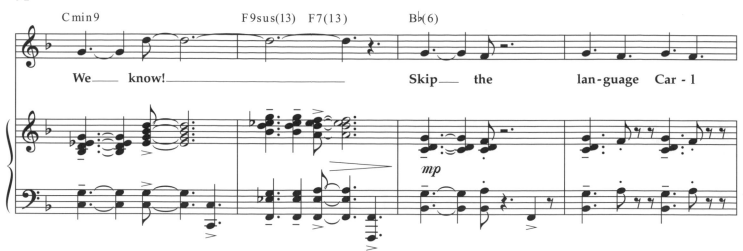

We know! Skip the lan-guage Car - l

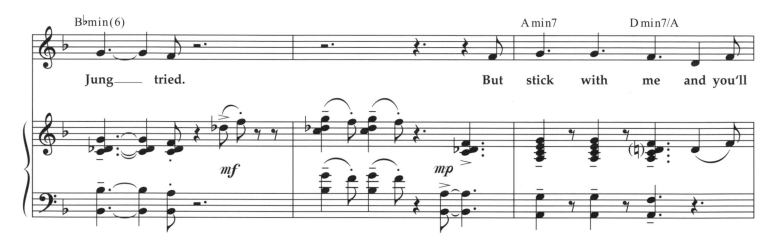

Jung tried. But stick with me and you'll

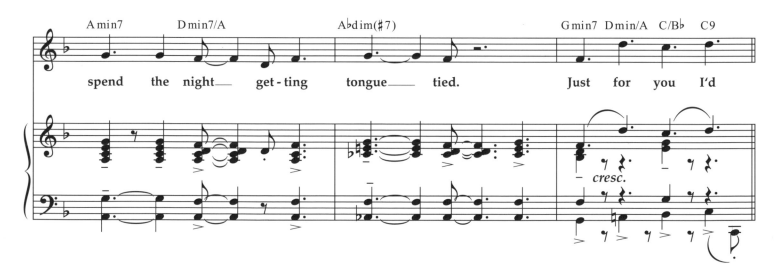

spend the night get-ting tongue tied. Just for you I'd

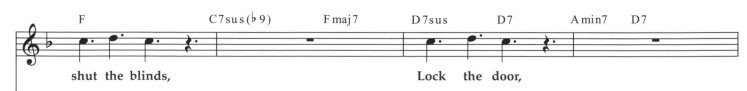

shut the blinds, Lock the door,

Serve you till you scream, "No more!"— of,— You know,— so,

what— do— you say...? Why— don't we give it a try—

— And run a - way?!—

You're The Best Thing That Ever Happened To Me

from the Musical The IT Girl

Lyrics by
BT McNICHOLL

Music by
PAUL McKIBBINS

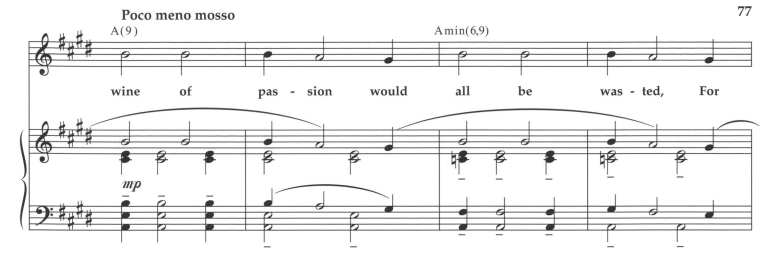

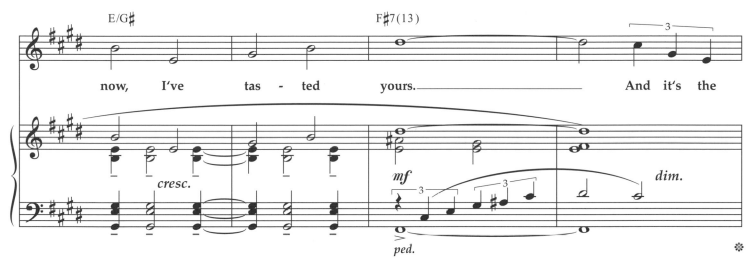

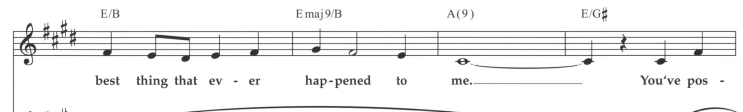

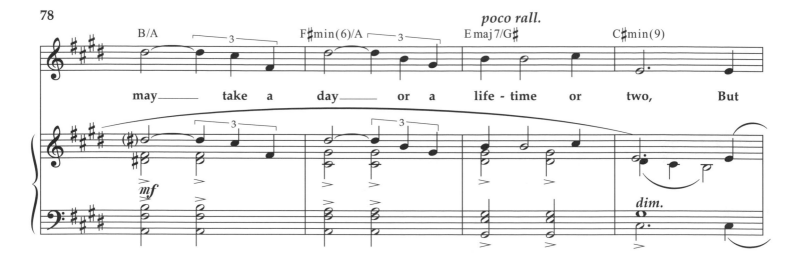

may take a day or a life-time or two, But

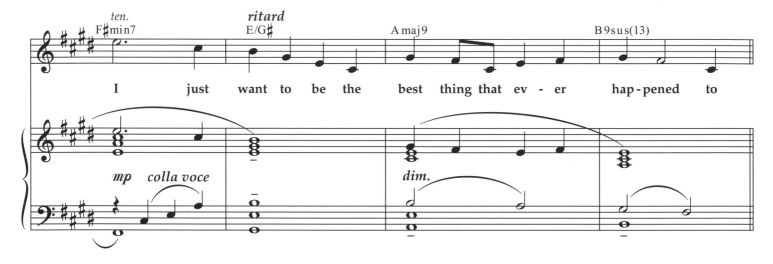

I just want to be the best thing that ev-er hap-pened to

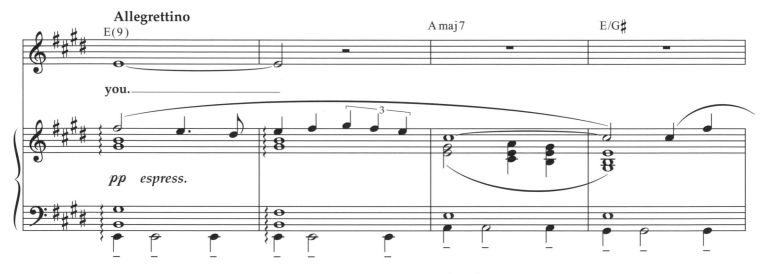

you.

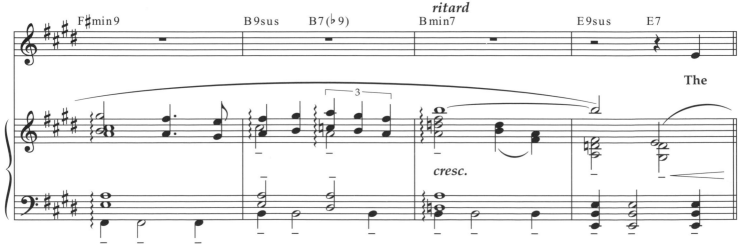

The

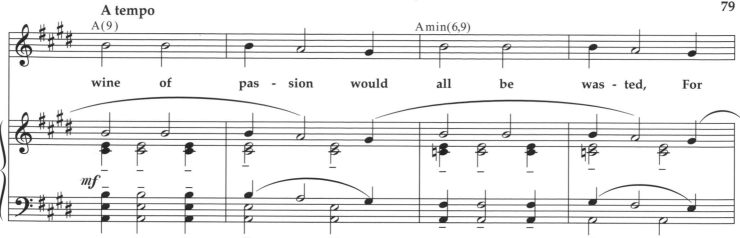

A tempo

A(9)　　　　　　　　　　　　Amin(6,9)

wine of pas - sion would all be was - ted, For

E/G♯　　　　　　　　　F♯7(13)

now, I've tas - ted yours._____ And it's the

Emaj9/B　　　　　　　　　　　　　A(9)　　　　E/G♯

best thing that ev - er hap - pened to me._____ Let me

F♯min9　　　B9sus　　　　　Bmin7　　E7

live on the glow of love in your eyes!_____ It

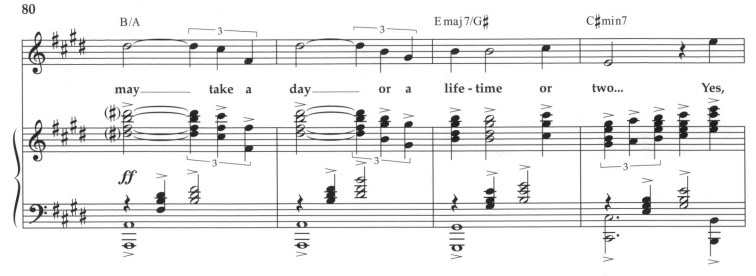

may take a day or a life-time or two... Yes,

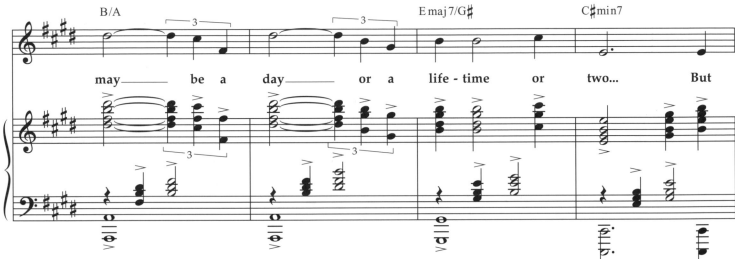

may be a day or a life-time or two... But

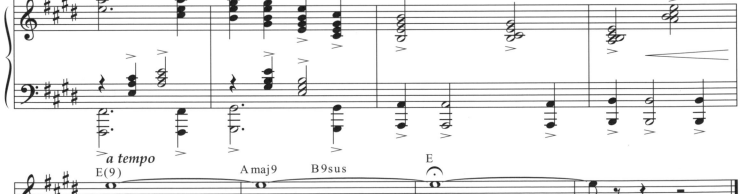

I won't rest till I'm the best thing that ev-er hap-pened to

you.